BASIC
RESCUE
AND
WATER
SAFETY

Third Edition 1984

American Red Cross

Preface

Safety in, on, and about the water depends on several factors. Ideally, every person who engages in any aquatic-related sport should know how to swim well. However, as more and more Americans take to the water in various kinds of activities, the percentage of good swimmers decreases alarmingly. Nonswimmers and novices by the thousands play in the water, fish, ski, and boat—and some even scuba dive. Inevitably, some drown.

Statistics on double drowning reflect the sad fact that many a nonswimming parent has drowned while trying to rescue a child, and many a youngster has overestimated his ability to help a friend in trouble in the water. The three major causes of drowning are, and always have been, failure to recognize hazardous conditions and practices, inability to get out of dangerous situations, and lack of knowledge of safe ways in which to aid drowning persons. It is in the hope of alleviating these problems that the Red Cross presents the information in this book.

Contents

BASIC WATER SAFETY

Drowning is the second leading cause of accidental death in the United States for persons from age 4 to age 44, exceeded only by motor vehicle accidents. More than 7,000 persons drown annually, 4,700 of whom did not even intend to get wet. Two-thirds of those who drown do not know how to swim, while half are alone at the time of the accident. Many drownings could be avoided if someone nearby were to apply some basic rescue techniques that are within the capability of most persons to perform. Aquatic emergencies are frequent in this country, yet rarely is the average person aware of ways in which he—even if he is a nonswimmer —may safely assist in such a situation. To correctly respond in an aquatic emergency is something that can be learned, and the means to implement an effective, safe rescue are literally at our fingertips.

There are many assists from shore that can be safely carried out by a nonswimmer. Lying flat on the deck or pier and extending an arm to a struggling victim is one of the safest assists of all and could save many lives if used. There are various ways for persons to extend their reach while remaining on the deck, and additional rescue possibilities are open to those who can wade to a person in trouble in the water.

There are several basic principles that contribute to the safety of an unskilled rescuer, one of the most important being proper assessment of the situation. Sometimes a frightened victim can be "talked" ashore with encouraging words, often with greater safety than if a novice attempted a rescue in any other way. However, if a rescue is to be attempted, the environment must be considered, as well as the ability of the potential rescuer.

The position of the rescuer must assure continued safety, and he or she must have a firm grasp on some stable support. Where water depth is known and bottom conditions permit, wading rescues can be made in safety by nonswimmers, and novices with some swimming ability can use equipment for safe assists.

Assists

EXTENSION ASSISTS

Accidents frequently happen within arm's length of shore or a pier, and a nonswimmer or a novice may safely effect a rescue by lying flat on the deck, and, being careful to maintain his own balance, extending an arm to the victim (Fig. 1).

Fig. 1

If the victim is just out of reach, clothing or a towel may be used as a means of extending the reach of the rescuer. Another method of extending the reach is to use a pole, a tree branch, or an oar (Fig. 2), bringing it to the victim's side through the water. Allow the victim to grasp one end of the extended article and then pull him to safety. Do not let the victim pull you into the water.

Fig. 2

A shepherd's crook is available at most pools and may be used effectively as an extension assist, even if a victim is too frightened to grasp it. It is possible for a nonswimmer to make a deep-water rescue from the deck using this device.

If a rescuer needs to further lengthen his reach, he may enter the water, maintaining a tight grip on a firm support such as a ladder or a pier, and extend an arm through the water to a victim. If the victim is beyond reach, the rescuer may extend his whole body through the water so that the victim may grasp the rescuer's legs (Fig. 3).

Fig. 3

Reaching assists from small craft must be made with care, so as not to upset the craft or pull the rescuer into the water. Extend an oar, paddle, or water ski to the victim, pull him slowly alongside the boat so that he can grasp the stern (Fig. 4), and then row the boat to safety.

Fig. 4

THROWING ASSISTS

If a victim is beyond reach by any extension, a throwing assist with a ring buoy may be made. A ring buoy on a line should be kept aboard all small craft and should be prominently displayed at all private pools and farm ponds. In using it, the rescuer holds the coiled line in one hand, throws the buoy beyond the victim, and then pulls the victim slowly to shore (Fig. 5).

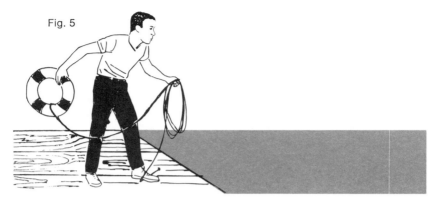

Fig. 5

If no buoy is available, a line may be thrown (Fig. 6) or, better still, a line to which has been attached a plastic jug containing a small amount of water for stability.

Fig. 6

Many items will float and provide some support for a person having difficulty in the water. Examples are a spare tire, a picnic chest, and a large thermos jug. Remember, if you cannot swim, it is futile to jump into the water yourself; a floatable object may give the victim all the support needed, until you can find a safe way to provide additional assistance. A Coast Guard approved buoyant cushion is a throwable device that will give maximum support. Families engaging in aquatic recreation should practice the use of such devices.

WADING ASSISTS

A nonswimmer may make a wading assist where necessary, if adequate precautions are made for the rescuer's own safety. The rescuer's body position is important; the body must be kept inclined toward shore, rather than toward the victim, so that the rescuer will not be pulled off balance (Fig. 7). Once the rescuer has made contact with the victim, the victim should be drawn slowly toward shore.

Fig. 7

Several rescuers may form a "human chain," to wade to a victim further from shore. Wrists must be tightly gripped, and movement toward shore must be careful and slow (Figs. 8A and 8B).

Fig. 8 A

Fig. 8 B

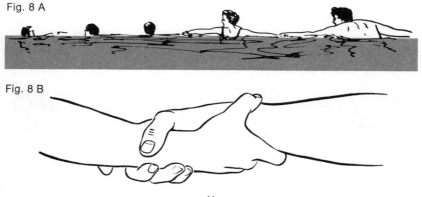

It is wise, where possible, to push or throw a floating object to a person in trouble in the water. Anything that floats can be useful: a board, a log, a kickboard, an inner tube, etc. (Fig. 9). A Coast Guard approved personal flotation device may also be used in this way. This kind of temporary support will give the victim relief while you search for a way to bring him ashore or to your boat.

Fig. 9

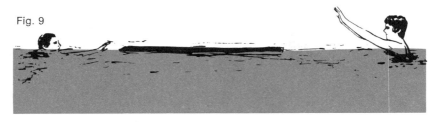

SWIMMING ASSISTS BY THE NOVICE

Some fundamental swimming skills are necessary before anyone can attempt a water rescue. Absolutely essential to the potential rescuer are the skills of treading water, survival floating, ability to disrobe in the water if necessary (plus the knowledge *not* to disrobe if the water is cold), and comfortable mobility in the water. Without these fundamental skills, a potential rescuer is only too likely to become, with the original victim, a double-drowning statistic. If an untrained person can swim comfortably and execute the other skills mentioned, he may then attempt simple rescues that involve swimming and use of equipment but do not require the rescuer to support or carry a victim through the water. Equipment that is lightweight and buoyant is best: a ring buoy, an inner tube, or an air mattress. Important things to remember are as follows:

1. Watch the victim as you approach (Fig. 10).

Fig. 10

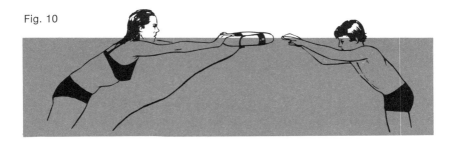

2. Keep the equipment between you and the victim.
3. Keep calm and calm the victim by talking to him if you can.

12

4. Once the victim has grasped the equipment, slowly pull him to shore (Fig. 11).

Fig. 11

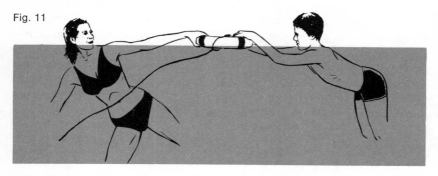

5. If the victim panics and climbs across the device toward you, *release* the equipment and swim away. Do not let the panicked victim grab you.

A novice swimmer can make a good, safe rescue by taking a ring buoy to the victim, while an assistant on shore retains one end of the line and then pulls both rescuer and victim to shore.

Ice Rescue

Ice strength depends upon thickness, snow cover, fluctuations in temperature, depth of water under the ice, current, and water level. In general, participants in ice sports should remember the following:

- Ice clouded with air bubbles should be avoided. It is usually weak.
- Skaters should not go near partially submerged obstacles such as stumps and rocks, where ice is weaker.
- Ice over moving water is likely to be unsafe.
- The ice should be examined for man-made hazards—holes where ice has broken or has been cut, for example. Such hazards should be well marked with a tree branch or similar object.

When an attempt is made to rescue someone who has fallen through ice, it is important for the rescuer to protect himself from danger. Any device that helps to distribute the weight of the rescuer over a wide area will lessen the possibility that the ice will continue to break.

A useful device for ice rescue is a light ladder, from 14 to 18 feet long, with a light, strong line attached to the lowest rung. The ladder should be shoved out on the ice to the limit of its length, with the line serving as an extension. If the victim has adequate strength, he may grasp the rungs and move prone along the ladder to safety. If this action is impossible, the rescuer may move prone along the ladder to the victim (Fig. 12) and grasp the victim's wrists or armpits, and both rescuer and victim may then be pulled to safety by the attached line. If the ice breaks under the ladder, the ladder will angle upward from the broken-ice area and can be drawn to safety by other persons.

Fig. 12

Other usable rescue devices are buoys, ropes, sticks, poles, tree branches, and even a human chain of rescuers lying prone on the ice (Fig. 13). A

Fig. 13

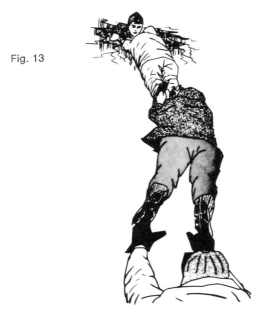

small flat-bottom boat may be shoved along the ice and will afford safety to the rescuer as the victim is pulled in over the stern (Fig. 14). Victims of skating and other ice accidents may require artificial respiration, which should be administered on the way to shelter, and may need warming and treatment for shock as well.

Fig. 14

Personal Flotation Devices

Federal law requires that there be a Coast Guard approved personal flotation device (Fig. 15) for each person afloat in a small craft. Common sense dictates that the device be *worn,* by nonswimmers and novices especially. The ability to don and use a personal flotation device (PFD) is a skill that can be learned and practiced easily in water of standing depth. With straps fastened securely, a buoyant vest can maintain proper position in the water for swimmer and nonswimmer alike, and mobility can be acquired easily by kicking and moving arms in "dog paddle" fashion. A PFD may be used under the arms for support in the water even without being worn. When aboard a small craft, or when fishing from a pier or shore, all nonswimmers and novices should wear a PFD.

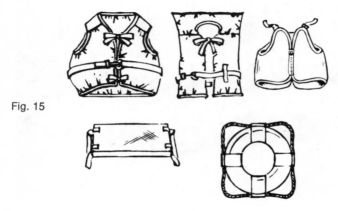

Fig. 15

Care of Victims With Neck and Back Injuries

Potential injury to the spinal cord should always be considered in any accident involving the neck or back. Careful handling of the victim is extremely important to prevent injury or possible further injury. Keep the victim's head, neck, and back in alignment as much as possible. In a water accident, it is especially important to keep the victim's entire body in alignment. There should be no extension, or if absolutely necessary, minimal extension, of the victim's neck if the victim requires artificial respiration or CPR.

A victim of a water accident must be floated to shore carefully, preferably on a firm, supportive object. Ideally, the victim should be handled only by trained personnel using proper equipment. If it is necessary to remove the victim from the water without trained assistance, remember that he should not be removed from the water until a rigid support is available. If no backboard is available, any rigid support may be adapted, such as a wooden door, a surfboard, an aquaplane, a wooden plank, and ironing board, or any similar item that will not break or bend. If the victim is floating face down, turn him over carefully with the least amount of movement, keeping his head and body aligned (Figs. 16A through 16C). Avoid making contact with the victim's head while turning him over. The victim can be floated on his back with minimal hand support (Fig. 16D). The backboard is placed under the victim by sliding it under the water and letting it float up (Fig. 17). Use any available material

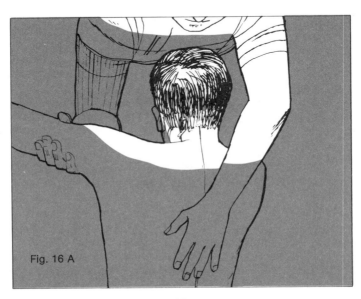

Fig. 16 A

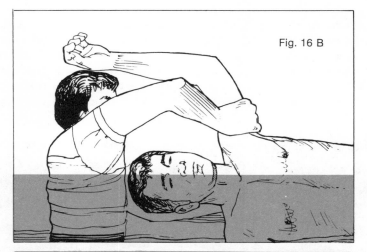

Fig. 16 B

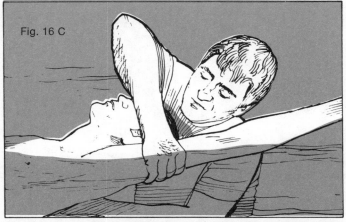

Fig. 16 C

Fig. 16 D

17

to secure the victim's body to the rigid support (Fig. 18). In removing the victim from the water, keep him as level as possible (Fig. 19). Extreme care in handling the victim of back and neck injuries is necessary to avoid the tragedy of permanent paralysis. Once on the deck, the victim is given first aid for shock and his breathing and circulation are monitored until emergency medical personnel arrive (Fig. 20).

Fig. 17

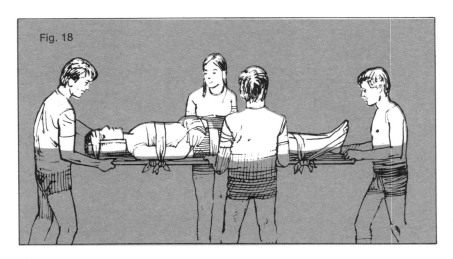
Fig. 18

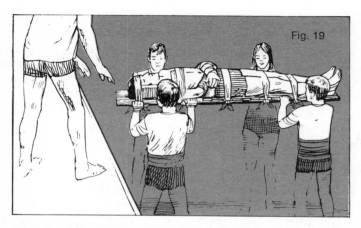

Fig. 19

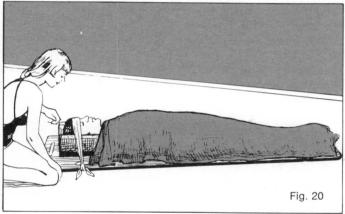

Fig. 20

Boating Safety

Personal safety while in, on, or about the water is directly related to the individual's swimming ability. Users of small craft should be able to swim at least 10 minutes fully clothed. Those who cannot do so should wear a Coast Guard approved personal flotation device (PFD) at all times when aboard small craft. Persons who feel at home in the water are not likely to panic in case of an accidental dunking but are able to plan and execute a logical sequence of steps toward safeguarding or rescuing themselves or others.

BOARDING AND DEBARKING

Procedures for correctly entering and leaving small craft will differ somewhat, depending on the size and type of craft and how it is moored. There are, however, two fundamental principles of safety a person should apply: (1) keep your center of gravity low and (2)

19

correctly distribute your weight. Entering or leaving a canoe calls for some agility and a sense of balance. When the canoe is alongside a pier, enter it at a point near amidships. Stand or kneel near the edge of the pier, facing the bow. Grasp the gunwale with the near hand and place the foot that is nearer the canoe on the bottom, directly over the center line. Shift hands to both gunwales and transfer the body weight to the foot in the canoe. Bring the other foot aboard. Slide the hands along the gunwales and, keeping the weight low, move to the paddling position.

CAPSIZE PROCEDURE

Overboard practice or self-rescue techniques should come early in learning canoeing skills. Experienced canoeists seldom fall overboard because they normally paddle from a kneeling position. However, beginners perched high on a seat or a thwart frequently find themselves in the water. This falling out often happens without capsizing or swamping the canoe; consequently, the ability to reenter a canoe from deep water is an important safety skill. There are several ways to reenter, but the easiest for most people is to reach over the gunwale near amidships (Fig. 21A), place the hands on the bottom of the canoe, press down with the hands, and kick the feet to the sur-

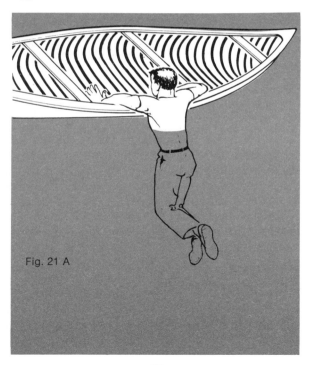

Fig. 21 A

face (Fig. 21B). The hands should continue to press down, and the feet should kick until the canoe is under the trunk of the body. The head should be kept low, and, when it is against the far side of the canoe, the body should roll over into a sitting position on the canoe's bottom (Fig. 21C).

Fig. 21 B

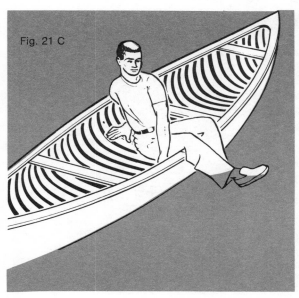

Fig. 21 C

Enter the swamped canoe in the same way as reentering an empty canoe (Fig. 22), but before bringing your legs aboard, remain in an athwart-ship position for a few seconds with your legs hanging over the gunwales (Fig. 23). This action will prevent the canoe from rolling and will also allow it to regain its proper floating position.

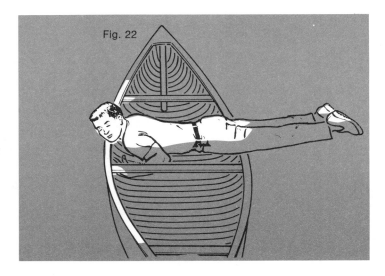

Fig. 22

Keep your weight as low as possible while your body does a quarter turn and your legs are brought aboard (Fig. 23).

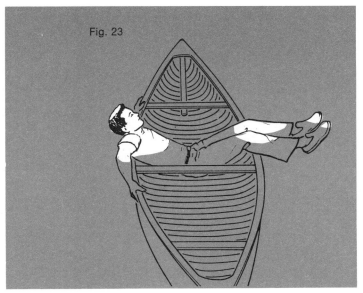

Fig. 23

From a sitting position in the bottom, paddle or hand-paddle the canoe to safety (Fig. 24).

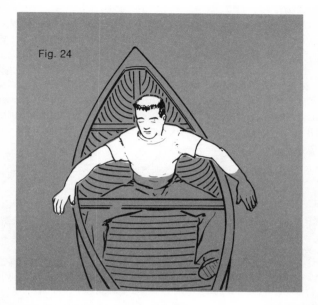

Fig. 24

There is danger in falling overboard if a canoeist is alone. Even a moderate breeze will blow a light canoe over the water faster than most people can swim. A panic-stricken person who has fallen overboard could quickly exhaust himself by trying to catch the canoe. It would be wiser to disrobe or to inflate the clothing and swim slowly toward shore, resting frequently by floating to conserve strength.

As a general rule, in case of capsizing or swamping, stay with the canoe and use it as a life raft. Only when the craft is drifting or being carried by the current toward dangerous waters (such as waterfalls, dams, and breaking surf), or when the water temperature is extremely cold, would it be prudent to attempt to swim for shore. You can use flotation gear or inflated clothing when you may have to leave the craft.

A capsized rowboat may also be used as a life raft, since it can be sighted more readily by rescuers than a lone swimmer. Roll it over into an upright position and salvage any loose gear that may be floating about. If there are extra buoyant cushions or life preservers, jam them under the thwarts or seats, where they will provide additional buoyancy. The boat can be entered from opposite sides when there are two or more persons, but the body weight should be mostly waterborne during the process to avoid rolling the boat over into a capsize position. Enter near amidships by reaching over the gunwale and placing your hands on the bottom. Kick your feet to the surface of the water and slide over the gunwale (Fig. 25). The hands partially support the body weight. When your hips clear the gunwale, do a half-roll and sit on the bottom with your legs trailing over the side (Fig. 26). If there is a tendency for the boat to roll, the weight of your legs will stabilize the craft by acting as outriggers. Your shoulders should be kept beneath the surface of the water if the boat's margin of buoyancy is low.

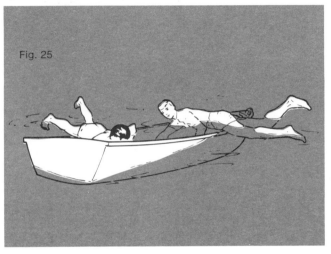

Fig. 25

Fig. 26

When the balance has been established and the boat has leveled off in its floating position, slide your legs aboard and adjust the athwartship trim by moving to one side or the other. The boat can then be paddled to shore, using either the oars or the hands (Fig. 27).

Fig. 27

Most outboard hulls are designed to float in case of a capsize; usually, there is sufficient buoyancy to support the partially submerged weight of motor and crew. Wooden hulls and those that have flotation compartments up under the deck and along the gunwale line will float upright though full of water and can be used as life rafts.

Any family engaging in small craft activity would be wise to invest some time in taking small craft safety courses. Actual practice of small craft safety techniques in controlled class situations greatly increases enjoyment and safety in family recreation.

Artificial Respiration

A respiratory emergency is an emergency in which normal breathing stops or in which breathing is so reduced that oxygen intake is insufficient to support life. The average person may suffer irreversible brain damage in 4 minutes or less if his circulation is cut off. Since it is often impossible to tell exactly when a person has stopped breathing, artificial respiration should be started as rapidly as possible. The mouth-to-mouth technique of artificial respiration is the most practical and effective method for emergency ventilation of a person of any age who has stopped breathing. A non-

25

breathing victim may need to be given cardiopulmonary resuscitation (CPR). Red Cross publications about respiratory and circulatory emergencies are available for purchase for nominal fees from your Red Cross chapter. Contact your chapter about these publications and for information about CPR courses.

The ABC's of Family Water Safety

It has often been said that accidents do not just happen—they are caused. Furthermore, the accident that happens today may have been caused a few weeks ago, by inadequate planning for safety. For example, the drowning of a youngster on a canoe trip may not really be caused when the canoe overturns and the child panics and sinks; it may have been caused when, for whatever reason, the youngster did not plan ahead to wear a personal flotation device.

Family outings can sometimes become family tragedies, unless there is preparation for safety. The following suggestions are an "alphabet for safety."

- **Accidents** are the leading cause of death for persons from age 1 to age 44 in the United States, and drownings annually claim about 7,000 lives. On the average, there are 13 accidental deaths and 1,300 disabling injuries every hour during the year.

- **Barefoot** on the beach is lots of fun, but watch out for broken glass, sharp rocks, and other objects that might cause painful cuts and bruises.

- **Camping** near the water? Make sure it's a safe swimming place before you swim. A firm sand or gravel bottom with a gradual slope and no stepoffs is most safe, but make sure there are no underwater obstructions.

- **Diving** into unknown water or into shallow-breaking waves is dangerous. Don't risk it.

- **Electric** storms in the area? Stay out of the water. Get under protective cover, such as a building. If you are in a small boat, head for shore.

- **First** aid courses are preparation for safety. Plan ahead—be prepared—take a first aid course.

- **Guarded** areas are best for swimming, but remember that even when there are lifeguards, your children are your responsibility.

- **H**ome pool on your property? Safety is your responsibility. There are at least 500 drownings in home pools annually. The main contributory causes of pool accidents are (1) lack of supervision, (2) inadequate barriers, and (3) inability to swim.

- **I**nflated tubes, air mattresses, etc., provide fun in the water—but often danger as well. Nonswimmers and novices should never be allowed in deep water with such devices.

- **J**ellyfish and other marine life can cause painful wounds and toxic reactions. Learn what to expect in an area *before* you decide to swim there.

- **K**now your limitations. Many people get in trouble in the water because they overestimate their swimming ability.

- **L**earn to swim. You can't think of a better sport to save your life.

- **M**outh-to-mouth artificial respiration should be given at the earliest possible moment to nonbreathing victims of submersion. Learn this lifesaving procedure. Be prepared!

- **N**ever swim alone, no matter how well you swim. Swim with a buddy.

- **O**verheated? It's no time to swim. Cool off a bit and then enjoy a swim.

- **P**FD's are personal flotation devices, which should be *worn* by nonswimmers and novices aboard small craft? Do you have a handicapped child in your family? How well will the child be able to care for himself in an emergency? Shouldn't the child wear a PFD? Think about it—and make sure the PFD is a Coast Guard approved device.

- **Q**ualified instructors of skin and scuba diving can teach you how to enjoy this sport in safety. Don't "pick up the sport on your own"; learn from qualified instructors.

- **R**eaching assists are the safest methods of rescue, for both the rescuer and the victim. Reach with an arm, a leg, a pole, a towel, a branch, an oar, a paddle, or a ski.

- **S**unburn can spoil a day of fun. If you're planning an all-day canoe trip, an outing at the beach, or a similar day in the sun, take along something with which to cover up.

- **T**ides move large masses of water and can create currents of considerable force. Never try to "buck" a current; swim diagonally toward shore.

- **U**nderwater swimming is both enjoyable and challenging, but do it for short distances only. Don't hyperventilate before swimming underwater, diving, or testing how long the breath can be held underwater. Hyperventilation can cause mental confusion and "blackouts."

- **V**acations—plain or fancy, long or short—are lots of fun, but don't let an accident spoil your vacation. Think safe, act safe, and be safe.

- **W**ater where you swim should be clear and unpolluted, free of debris, comfortable in degree of temperature, and preferably without current.

- **X**tra safety preparation means an "Xtra"-safe vacation.

- **Y**ou can help, even if you can't swim. Reach, throw, or row—but don't go.

- **Z**ero in on safety; you'll be glad you did.

BASIC RESCUE

Safety in the water is largely a personal matter. All persons who engage in aquatic activities should steadily acquire the knowledge and skill that will enable them to take care of themselves under all except the most unusual conditions. As individuals increase their aquatic skill, there should be a parallel development of personal safety skills that will enable them to meet emergencies if they arise.

There are literally millions of swimming places in the United States, ranging in type from the "old swimming hole" variety to the modern swimming pool facility. Obviously, one of the first principles of water safety is to choose a safe place in which to swim. Common sense should guide the swimmer to select a site that is designed for swimming and that provides the protection of lifeguards. If there are no such sites, a person should consider the many factors of a safe swimming area before selecting a place to swim. Rivers, ponds, quarries, lakes, and ocean beaches where swimming is unsupervised all have certain hazards. In a safe swimming area, the water should be clear and free from pollution. The bottom should slope gently toward deep water, with no holes, step-offs, hidden obstructions, or debris. The area should be free of dangerous marine life or be protected from it. Decks and piers should be of sturdy construction and have a nonslippery surface. Wooden piers should be closely planked.

Some hazards in the aquatic environment stem from the swimmers themselves. For example, novices who overestimate their ability may find themselves unable to return to shore owing to exhaustion; a sudden cramp may cause a swimmer to need help.

There are three basic rules for personal safety in emergencies: Do not panic. Think. Save your strength.

Specific Emergencies

CRAMPS

The majority of cramps experienced in the water will be those that affect the hands, feet, arms, or legs and are usually caused by fatigue or overexertion. Cramps are of little danger to swimmers unless they cause them to panic. If swimmers change their stroke and relax, this

29

action alone will, in many cases, bring relief. If the cramp continues, rubbing and kneading may help (Fig. 36), but most important is the stretching of the muscle. If initiated as soon as a swimmer feels a distinct twitch or warning sign, the stretching process and a change of stroke will usually bring relief.

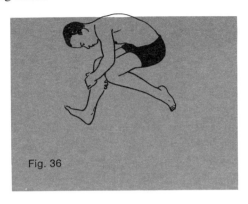
Fig. 36

CURRENTS

When caught in a current, a swimmer should not attempt to buck or fight it. Instead, he should swim diagonally across the current. Even though this action may bring the swimmer farther downstream, it will enable him to reach safety without being exhausted.

RUNOUTS AND RIP CURRENTS

Runouts and rip currents tend to drag the swimmer away from the shore. The swimmer should not panic or struggle. Instead, he should swim parallel to shore across the current and, once free, should swim to shore.

WEEDS

When caught in weeds, the victim should not thrash or make a quick, vigorous movement. Use of slow, careful movements will help to prevent further entanglement. A slow arm movement with just a gentle waving action of the legs is recommended.

Disrobing in the Water

A majority of drownings occur when people find themselves accidentally in the water and fully clothed. In such cases, the knowledge of how to disrobe in the water can be vitally important. The weight of water-soaked clothing impairs swimming efficiency, but in some instances it might be best not to disrobe. When safety is only a short distance away or there is the problem of cold water or when it is possible to safely hang onto a buoyant object, it might not be advisable to disrobe.

If the swimmer realizes that shirts and trousers can be easily inflated and can act as flotation supports, it is readily seen that there is no need for panic. First of all, however, the swimmer should remove his shoes. To accomplish this he takes a good breath and assumes a jellyfish float position. Then using both hands, he removes one shoe at a time (Fig. 37). When necessary, he should lift his head long enough to take additional breaths as needed during this procedure.

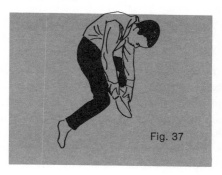

Fig. 37

Use of Clothing for Flotation

Close-woven materials that most shirts and slacks are made from hold trapped air when wet. The shirt can be inflated to give initial support. First, it is buttoned at the collar and made tight at the neck. Then the swimmer takes a deep breath, bends the head forward, pulls the shirt up to the face, and exhales between the second and third buttons (Fig. 38). The air will rise and form a bubble at the back of the shirt and give the needed support. It may be necessary to grasp the shirt collar tightly to prevent the escape of the trapped air.

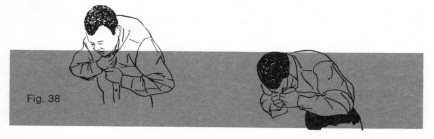

Fig. 38

Another method of inflating a shirt is by splashing air into it with the palm of the hand. To accomplish this skill, the swimmer floats on the back and holds the front of the shirttail with one hand, keeping it just under the surface. The free hand strikes downward from above the surface with the palm and continues the motion to a point below the shirttail. The air, carried downward from the surface, will bubble into the shirt, causing the inflation.

To use slacks for flotation, the swimmer takes a good breath, assumes a jellyfish float position, loosens the waistband or belt, and carefully and easily removes one leg of the clothing at a time (Fig. 39A). The head should be lifted high enough to enable the swimmer to take a breath as often as necessary. It is important not to hurry.

After the slacks are removed, the swimmer treads water and either ties both legs of the slacks together at the cuff or ties a knot in each leg as close to the bottom of the leg of the slacks as possible. Then, with the zipper pulled up, the swimmer grasps the back of the waistband with one hand and, with the slacks on the surface, splashes air into the open waist with the free hand. This procedure is carried out by striking downward with the palm and following through to a point just below the open waist, which is kept below the surface (Fig. 39B).

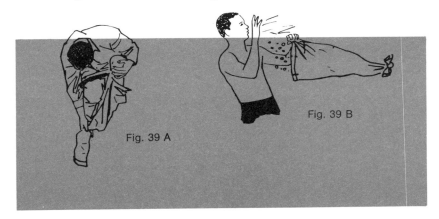

Fig. 39 A

Fig. 39 B

Another simple method of inflating slacks is to submerge and blow air into them through the waistband, which should be kept underwater. After the slacks have been inflated, the waistband can be gathered together by the hands or by tightening the belt if there is one. The swimmer can then slip his head between the legs of the slacks near where they have been tied together, thus forming a Mae West type of flotation device. If the legs are tied separately, the swimmer uses the inflated trousers as waterwings, which would be an equally serviceable improvised flotation support (Fig. 40).

Fig. 40

Survival Floating

The face-down floating technique described below is adapted from the "drownproofing" technique that was originated by the late Fred R. Lanoue, former professor of physical education and head swimming coach at the Georgia Institute of Technology. This style of floating combines a series of basic swimming skills and is designed to keep a person afloat for hours with a minimum of effort.

The skill of survival floating can be performed as follows:

1. Resting position

    The swimmer starts with air in the lungs and, holding the breath, lets arms and legs dangle. The face is kept down so that the back of the head is at the surface. The swimmer rests and floats in this position for a few seconds (Fig. 41).

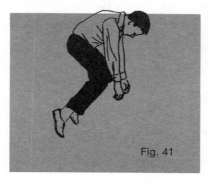

Fig. 41

2. Preparing to exhale

While maintaining the resting position, the swimmer slowly and un-hurriedly recovers, or lifts, the arms to about shoulder height. If leg action is also to be used, the swimmer slowly separates the legs into a modified scissors kick (Fig. 42).

Fig. 42

3. Exhalation

Making sure that the back of the head is still at the surface, the swimmer raises the head no higher than necessary for the mouth to clear the surface. At the same time, the swimmer exhales through the mouth and nose. (Some people may exhale through mouth only or nose only.) The eyes should be opened to help gauge the head and body levels (Fig. 43).

Fig. 43

4. Inhalation

As soon as the swimmer's head is vertical, he presses the arms downward and brings the legs together. This easy downward pressure should allow time for air to be breathed in through

34

the mouth. The action of the arms and legs should not be vigorous enough to lift the chin out of the water (Fig. 44).

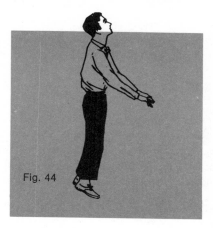

Fig. 44

5. Return to the resting position

The swimmer slowly allows the arms and legs to move back to their free-dangling position, with face down in the water, and relaxes (Fig. 45). The swimmer rests in this position until ready to exhale and then repeats the cycle. NOTE. If the individual tends to sink too far below the surface when going back to the dangling, or resting, position, a downward press or easy finning action of the arms will stop the sinking of the body and help float it back to the surface. A slight scissors kick can also be combined to arrest the sinking action.

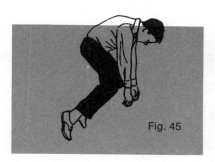

Fig. 45

Swimming Skills for Basic Rescue

Although a person trained in basic rescue must never attempt to approach or carry a struggling, panicked victim, the basic rescuer can, with some adaptation of swimming strokes, recover and tow an unconscious victim. There are obvious problems in executing this task.

The rescuer must accept the handicap of swimming not only for himself but also for the victim. This added burden is further complicated by the fact that one arm must be used for holding the victim. The rescuer's legs, therefore, must be stroking with maximum effectiveness and power. The sidestroke, or scissors, kick has proven to be the most effective leg action for most people in towing a victim. However, in some instances, a swimmer who has an effective, powerful breaststroke kick may prefer that method.

In most instances, it is necessary to invert the scissors kick in order to allow for the changed body position and to avoid kicking the victim, although either the standard or the inverted scissors kick may be used. In the standard scissors kick, the top leg is extended laterally forward (Fig. 46). In the inverted scissors kick, the top leg is extended laterally backward (Fig. 47).

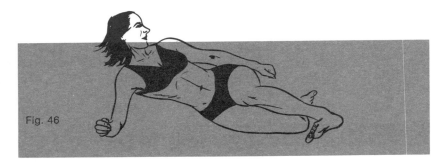

Fig. 46

Fig. 47

The arm pull of the sidestroke must be adapted somewhat, eliminating the glide and making the action somewhat shorter and faster. The direction of pull is essentially the same as in the regular sidestroke, with the hand and bent arm pressing backward toward the feet.

Search and Rescue

SURFACE DIVES

For the rescuer to assist in search and rescue, some additional aquatic skills are necessary. The ability to surface dive from a swimming position on the surface of the water to moderate underwater depths is a skill that is often used for personal enjoyment. It is especially useful for rescuing submerged victims.

In the early stages of development, the learner should not dive deeper than from 6 to 8 feet. As skill and physical adjustment to water pressure improve, the swimmer can attempt slightly deeper dives.

Pike Surface Dive

As the name implies, the pike surface dive (Fig. 48) is performed with the legs in an extended position throughout the dive. Prior to initiating

Fig. 48

the dive, the swimmer comes to a position of full extension on the surface. Then, while still having momentum, the swimmer takes a breath and presses the arms back in a broad, sweeping, continuous motion toward the thighs. The beginning arm action is similar to the breaststroke movement but does not stop at the shoulders. This arm action, combined with a flexing at the hips, will bring the head underwater almost directly under the hips. At this point and without pause, the arms are circled forward vigorously, bringing the palms into a streamlined diving position, facing downward and together. The lifting of the extended legs occurs as part of both the reaction to this forward press of the arms and the extension of the hips. The body is then in a fully extended and streamlined position directed toward the bottom at a slight angle from the vertical. If these actions have been properly performed, the weight of the legs in this altered position should result in driving the body to a depth of about 8 feet without additional stroking of the arms and legs.

Exhaling gently through the nose during the dive will result in maintaining positive pressure and will prevent water from entering the nasal passages.

Feetfirst Surface Dive

The feetfirst, or feet-foremost, dive (Fig. 49) is a method of diving deeply into murky water of unknown depth or bottom condition. Since the initial part of the dive involves a feetfirst descent, it is essential to raise the body sufficiently above the surface to provide the necessary weight to start its downward plunge. To do this, the swimmer first assumes the vertical position for treading water.

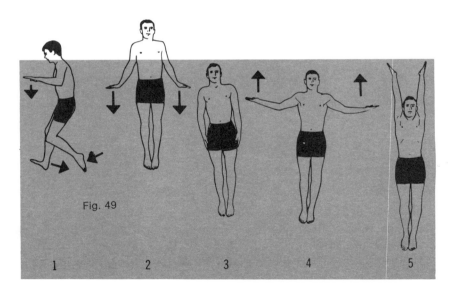

Fig. 49

1   2   3   4   5

The swimmer then presses downward, with the hands going all the way to the sides, while executing a vigorous breaststroke kick or scissors kick. When the upper part of the body has risen to its highest point out of water, the body is streamlined by holding the arms at the side, legs extended, and toes pointed. When the head sinks below the surface, the wrists are rotated to turn the palms upward and outward and the hands press vigorously upward, thus preserving the downward momentum.

38

As in the other surface dives, gently exhaling throughout the descent is advisable. This action often plunges the swimmer to a depth of at least 10 feet. Depending on the reason for the dive and the condition of the water and the bottom, the swimmer may want to level off after the initial feetfirst downward plunge ceases, or he can perform a tuck surface dive and swim to greater depths.

UNDERWATER SWIMMING

The skill of underwater swimming enables swimmers to recover lost objects, avoid surface hazards, and enjoy underwater activities. Many drownings have been prevented through the ability of rescuers to surface dive and search the bottom by swimming underwater.

Swimmers with average skill rarely swim at depths greater than from 10 to 15 feet and should not go deeper except to perform an emergency rescue or, after long practice, to engage in skin diving or other underwater activities. Distance underwater swimming should be discouraged, and the dangers of hyperventilating the lungs before swimming underwater should be thoroughly understood. Hyperventilation, or deep breathing, increases breath-holding time by blowing off carbon dioxide and thus decreasing the amount of carbon dioxide in the blood. If, following hyperventilation, a person attempts to swim underwater for a distance, a considerable length of time may elapse before the carbon dioxide level, reduced by overbreathing, will provide a strong stimulus to breathe. The danger is that the oxygen level may drop to a point where the swimmer "blacks out" before the carbon dioxide level increases to the point where he feels the urge to take a breath. Unless help is at hand to get him to the surface, drowning will result. Every person engaged in underwater swimming should be paired with a buddy and should be closely supervised.

USE OF MASK, FINS, AND SNORKEL

It is necessary for the rescuer to have information concerning the use of mask, fins, and snorkel and the safety factors involved in the use of this equipment. These fundamental skills should be practiced under the guidance of a qualified instructor and will provide the student with knowledge necessary to assist in underwater search and recovery of unconscious victims. The skills presented here are fundamental. Those wishing to engage in the sport of skin diving are urged to enroll in a complete course of instruction offered by qualified scuba instructors.

Basic equipment used for underwater search and recovery consists of a mask, fins, and snorkel. The most important item is the mask, which provides visibility for the swimmer when swimming on the surface with the face in the water or when swimming underwater. The fins provide propulsion that enables the swimmer to cover large search areas quickly and with little effort. The snorkel allows the swimmer to breathe while swimming on the surface with the face in the water and is of great value when used with the mask to scan the bottom rapidly.

Mask

Masks (Fig. 50) should be constructed of soft, flexible rubber with an untinted, shatterproof safety glass facepiece, held in position by a corrosion-proof metal band. A single or a divided strap holds the mask in place and can be adjusted to fit the diver's head.

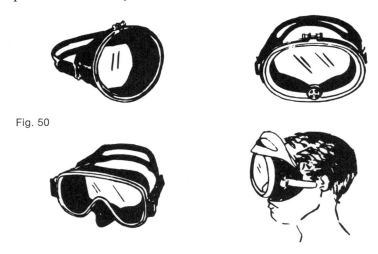

Fig. 50

Some masks are equipped with a purge valve, which allows the individual to clear water from the mask by exhaling through the nose.

Masks with a nose-blocking device, or with a molded indentation to fit the nose, enable the swimmer to block off or pinch the nose to equalize air pressure in the ear canal as he dives more deeply.

To test for proper fit, the swimmer places the mask against the face without applying the head strap. If the mask is properly sealed, when the swimmer inhales through the nose, the mask will stay in place without being held.

Fins

Fins (Fig. 51) are constructed in various ways. Some float; others do not. Some are designed with a full foot and are worn like a shoe; others are open at the heel and are held in position by a heel strap.

Fins should be selected so that they fit the feet properly to avoid chafing or cramping during use and should have the proper flexibility and blade size for the strength of the swimmer's kick.

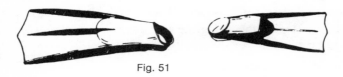

Fig. 51

Snorkel

Snorkels (Fig. 52) used by skilled swimmers are J-shaped rubber tubes from 12 to 15 inches in length. Some are molded in one piece, while others have a ribbed, flexible section for the curved portion of the tube. All are fitted with a soft rubber, flanged mouthpiece, which should be the right size for the user so that water cannot seep in as he breathes.

Fig. 52

Skill Practice

Although use of the equipment appears quite simple, it is, in reality, a skill that demands practice. In a class situation, and always with a buddy, the student should practice the skills described below.

Mask

1. Defogging faceplate
   To prevent the faceplate's fogging while being used underwater,

before putting it on, rub the inside of the glass with saliva, leaves, kelp, or glycerine and then rinse it off with water.

2. Putting on mask
   Place the mask over your face first and then pull the strap over your head. This procedure prevents getting hair between the mask and the face.

3. Checking for leaks and defogging effectiveness
   With the mask in place, submerge until your head is below the surface. If the mask leaks, come to the surface and adjust the straps. Repeat the defogging procedure if the glass continues to fog over.

4. Flooding and emptying mask
   Submerge and flood the mask by lifting an edge. Surface and empty the mask by raising the lower edge from your face. Submerge and flood the mask again. While in a horizontal swimming position, turn your head to one side to pocket the water on the lower side. Press the top side of the mask firmly to your face and exhale forcefully through your nose, forcing the water out under lower side of the mask.

5. Relieving mask pressure
   With the mask in position, submerge and exhale a little air through your nose. This will relieve mask face pressure as the depth of the dive increases.

6. Relieving ear pressure
   Ear pressure also increases as the diver goes deeper, and may cause some pain. This pressure may be relieved by pressing the mask against your face and exhaling through your nose, or by swallowing and moving your jaws. Masks equipped with a nose-blocking device or a molded nose indentation simplify the process of equalizing pressure.

Fins

1. Walking with fins
   Wet fins before putting them on. This makes them easier to pull on over the feet. When walking on land, lift your feet high to prevent tripping. Never run while wearing fins. When walking in the water wearing fins, walk backward. It is often better to walk out to deep water before putting on fins.

2. Kicking while wearing fins
   Use the crawl kick when swimming with fins. The kick should be

42

slower and deeper than when kicking without fins, with a greater knee bend. Always keep the fins in the water when you are kicking at or near the surface, so that maximum benefit can be derived from the fin action.

Snorkel

1. Securing snorkel
   Place the snorkel between the face mask strap and your head, or slip it through the snorkel loop strap attachment.

2. Holding mouthpiece
   Place the mouthpiece in your mouth and grip it with your teeth. The flange should be between lips and teeth.

3. Snorkel breathing
   With snorkel and mask in position, stand in chest-deep water with your face submerged and breathe through the snorkel. Be careful to keep the snorkel opening above water when practicing and when swimming on the surface.

4. Flooding and emptying snorkel
   Submerge and flood the snorkel. On returning to the surface, keep your face submerged and expel the water from the snorkel by *forceful* mouth exhalation. Inhale carefully after clearing, in the event that some water remains in the tube. Practice until you can carry out this skill repeatedly in comfort.

Swimming Practice

1. Swimming on the surface
   Breathing through the snorkel, with your arms by your sides and your face in the water, swim on the surface (Fig. 53). This is the normal swimming position for scanning the bottom when the water is clear and not too deep.

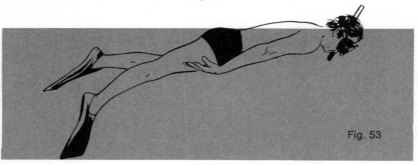
Fig. 53

2. Surface diving

As a safety procedure, after performing a surface dive, stop, look up, listen, and extend your hands overhead before surfacing (Fig. 54).

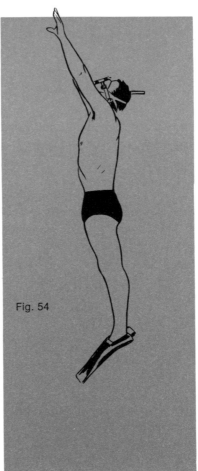

Fig. 54

3. Swimming underwater

The leg drive created by the fins makes arm stroking unnecessary when swimming underwater. Carry your arms forward for protection when swimming in unclear water.

4. Entering the water

Do not dive headfirst into the water from an elevation while wearing mask, fins, and snorkel. Hold the mask securely to your face and step off in a stride position. Some divers prefer to roll in if they are entering from a low elevation (Fig. 55).

Fig. 55

RELATED SAFETY INFORMATION FOR SKIN DIVING

- Before doing any diving, have a physical examination and get the doctor's approval to dive.

- Enroll in a complete course of instruction before diving in open-water areas.

- Always swim and dive with a buddy, never alone, and know where your buddy is at all times.

- Divers should be skilled swimmers and lifesavers. Minimum skills include being able to tread water, float, scull, surface dive, swim underwater, swim 440 yards using a stroke on the front and on the back, and perform a swimming rescue.

- In the early stages of learning, do not dive deeper than 10 feet. Remember that pressure increases rather rapidly as a diver descends. A broad guide of 1 pound of pressure per square inch for each 2 feet of descent emphasizes this pressure increase. For example, a depth of 16 feet would equal 8 pounds. This pressure added to the normal atmospheric pressure of 14.7 pounds totals 22.7 pounds of pressure on each square inch of the diver's body. It is this pressure that causes mask squeeze and ear pain.

- Hyperventilation, or deep breathing to prolong the diver's ability to stay underwater longer, should be discouraged. Hyperventilation increases the oxygen intake but lowers the carbon dioxide in the bloodstream. When the carbon dioxide content is lowered, bodily functions are altered, and mental confusion can result. The diver fails to recognize the usual signs that indicate his oxygen supply is exhausted and may lose consciousness while underwater. Unless help is available, he drowns.

- Do not wear earplugs when diving. During a dive, pressure differences in the ear canal caused by the earplugs and the water pressure can result in permanent ear damage.

- Do not wear goggles for diving purposes. Unlike relieving pressure with the face mask, there is no way of relieving pressure on goggles as the diver goes deeper, other than removing the goggles. Eye injuries can occur if the diver persists in diving to depths wearing goggles.

- An important safety practice when diving in open-water areas is to have a boat or some type of float close at hand. A boat is preferred. When a boat is not available, an improvised float can be made from a good innertube and a clothes basket or net material (Fig. 56) to provide a resting support for the diver and a receptacle in which to store articles. Boats or floats should be equipped with the proper anchor and a line long enough and strong enough to anchor them securely during high wind or wave action.

Fig. 56

- The inflatable vest (Fig. 57) is a valuable item for the safety of the

Fig. 57

skin diver and should be worn at all times when diving in open-water areas. The vest should be designed to inflate by cartridge and by mouth, for emergencies, and should support the diver's head with the face out of water. This support is very important if the diver should lose consciousness.

- The diver's flag (Fig. 58), which may be purchased or constructed, is a reddish-orange rectangle with a diagonal white stripe. It is flown from the diver's boat or float to warn craft in the area that a diver is below or in the vicinity. When displayed, the flag should be at least 3 feet above the surface to provide good visibility. Swimming and diving activities should be confined to within 100 feet of the flag.

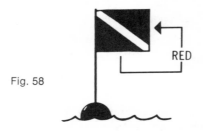

RED

Fig. 58

- The unskilled diver should avoid surging seas, swift currents, and murky water when skin diving. A diver should be alert to the possibility of dangerous marine life and growth. He or she should check with local skin diving groups for advice before diving in a new location.

- Avoid prolonged exposure to the water, particularly cold water. Fatigue and cold can cause cramps.

- Always stop, look up, reach up, and listen before surfacing after a dive.

- Do not allow small children to play with a mask while in the water. Lives have been lost because children, in placing the mask over their face, covered both the nose and mouth. With the mask in this position, the child's natural breathing creates a mask suction that cannot be released by the child, and he suffocates.

- Have a first aid kit available when skin diving. Gauze compresses, triangular bandages, adhesive compresses, scissors, and tweezers are a few of the items needed. All divers should complete a first aid course to learn how to care for injuries; local Red Cross chapters can provide this instruction.

Recovery of Submerged Victims

After becoming proficient at surface diving and underwater swimming, an individual may ably assist lifeguards in search and recovery of drowning victims and may himself recover an unconscious victim. If the rescuer knows approximately where the victim was last seen, he or she swims to that spot, does a quick surface dive, and locates the victim. Swimming behind the victim, the rescuer grasps the hair, chin, or collar of the unconscious person and by vigorous leg strokes makes his way to the surface. The rescuer may then tow the victim ashore by using one of several tows. If the rescuer must swim to the area where the victim is believed to be submerged, the swimming can be done with an easy stroke, so that the rescuer can conserve energy for the exacting effort of the underwater search and recovery.

SEARCH PROCEDURES

Approaching the target area, the rescuer should look for bubbles coming to the surface. If there are no telltale bubbles, the rescuer should swim along the surface, scanning the bottom with the aid of a mask. Against the dark bottom, the arms and legs of a victim, or contrasting clothing, can often be seen even if the water is deep. On a white sand bottom, the dark hair and bathing suit of a victim may show his position. Once the victim is located, the rescuer surface dives, swims behind him, and brings him to the surface as previously described.

SEARCH PATTERNS

If the position of the victim is not known, a systematic search of the bottom must be carried out, using a series of surface dives with short underwater swims. Choosing the area to be covered, the rescuer searches the bottom in overlapping lanes until the body is found or until he is satisfied that the victim is not in the area.

The rescuer covers two or three body lengths of the bottom on each underwater swim. Longer underwater swims are not advisable, since they only tire the rescuer.

Under some conditions it is not possible to locate the victim by sight, and it is necessary for the rescuer to swim close to the bottom, sweeping the arms ahead and to the side, in what has been termed "systematic groping."

If two or more rescuers are available, a greater area can be searched more rapidly. A line of several rescuers, doing parallel dives, can thoroughly cover a large area in the same time in which one diver can cover a narrow 4- or 5-foot strip. With lanes slightly overlapping, rescuers surface dive and take an agreed-upon number of underwater strokes. After each dive and short underwater swim, they surface, move back a body length, realign their group, and again dive and search (Fig. 59).

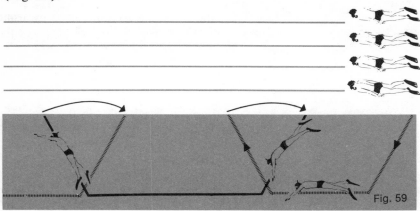

Fig. 59

When rescuers cannot locate the victim owing to poor visibility, bottom conditions, or depth of water, continued attempts should not be made. In such instances, the use of grappling apparatus is necessary.

APPROACH TO SUBMERGED VICTIM

Once a victim is located underwater, the rescuer surface dives, swims behind the victim, and grasps either the victim's chin, hair, or collar. The rescuer must then kick quite vigorously, in order to surface with the added weight of the victim. The inverted scissors kick is usually best for this purpose, although the swimmer with a strong breaststroke kick may utilize it effectively. If the victim is lying on the bottom, the rescuer may grasp an arm or clothing with a secure hold, to bring the victim to the surface.

TOWING THE UNCONSCIOUS VICTIM

Once on the surface, the victim may be towed ashore by utilizing any one of the tows illustrated below: the hair carry (Fig. 60), the shirt or collar tow (Fig. 61), or the wrist tow (Fig. 62).

Fig. 60

Fig. 61

Fig. 62

The rescuer utilizes the shallow arm pull and either the standard or the inverted scissors kick in towing an unconscious victim. Regardless of the tow used, the rescuer's grasp must be a very firm one. The rescuer should use a tow that maintains the victim's head above water if possible, and with which the rescuer can effectively make headway toward shore. In the event that the victim spontaneously regains consciousness, and his struggling makes progress toward shore impossible, the rescuer should release the hold and swim to safety. The rescuer must then decide upon an alternate method of rescue that can safely be used for a conscious, struggling victim.

Once an unconscious, nonbreathing victim is brought to shallow water, assistance may be required to get the person ashore. Two persons may bring an unconscious victim to the beach by grasping the victim's armpits and dragging him.

Since it is usually impossible to know how long a drowning victim has been unconscious, it is important to administer artificial respiration immediately. Mouth-to-mouth artificial respiration should be given as soon as possible—for example, in shallow water or in or alongside a boat. Once a victim of a near drowning has begun breathing for himself, he should be treated for shock and must receive medical attention.

In some drowning accidents, cardiopulmonary resuscitation (CPR) may have to be administered. All potential rescuers should have CPR training, which is available from Red Cross chapters.